For Family

By
Sylvia Gunter

Dedication

This book is humbly dedicated to all men and women, moms and dads, who desire to know God's Word, obey His will, pray His prayers, and glorify His name in your family. My prayer is that these prayer portions *For The Family* will encourage you to know our heavenly Father better, love Him more, and pray His heart for your family. There is no higher calling than to minister God's love and grace to your family through prayer.

This is a sampler of the intercessory prayer tools found in the "big blue book," *Prayer Portions*, 360 pages, 8-1/2" by 11" in size, containing 150 prayer resources. *Prayer Portions* contains sections on Praise, Repentance, Warfare, Personal Prayerlife, and Intercession. Half of these pieces are found there, but many are fresh from the refiner's fire of current "on-the-knees" experience. In our society, where the pace is ever faster and faster, the sheer size of *Prayer Portions* may be intimidating to those who haven't gotten started making prayer a way of life. *For The Family* is user-friendly for the "drive-thru window" generation. It is intended for two groups: those who need a vital starting point for a lifestyle of intercession for your family, and those who may be weary in prayer and need fresh weapons in the battle for your family.

You may order *Prayer Portions* and
For The Family from
The Father's Business, P. O. Box 380333, Birmingham, AL 35238.

Cover Design by Ben Fineburg
With special appreciation to the unsurpassed folks at AlphaGraphics
who are responsible for printing, cover design, order fulfillment service, and so much more.
Thanks to Rick, Iris, and your team. You're the best.
(AlphaGraphics, 3205 Lorna Road, #103, Hoover, AL 35216)

ISBN 1-931379-03-3

Contents

A Soldier's Prayer

I asked God for strength,
*   that I might achieve;*
I was made weak,
*   that I might humbly learn to obey.*

I asked for health,
*   that I might do greater things;*
I was given infirmity,
*   that I might do better things.*

I asked for riches,
*   that I might be happy;*
I was given poverty,
*   that I might be wise.*

I asked for power,
*   that I might have the praise of men;*
I was given weakness,
*   that I might feel the need of God.*

I asked for all things,
*   that I might enjoy life;*
I was given life,
*   that I might enjoy all things.*

I got nothing I asked for,
*   but everything I hoped for.*

Almost in spite of myself,
*   my unspoken prayers were answered.*

I among all men am most richly blessed.

These lines were written by an anonymous Confederate Soldier during the Civil War. As believers today, we are called to fight the good fight of faith. As you pray and obey, may God bless you as He did this soldier with rich knowledge of His ways.

Praying For The Family

Praying for your family is the most vital, unrelenting, frustrating, neglected, and rewarding assignment of a parent.

• **It is vital.** Your life and your family's may depend on it.

• **It is unrelenting.** It is daily. The enemy does not give up resisting the will of God for His children. That is the name and nature of our adversary— accuser, opposer, destroyer, thief, deceiver, liar, setter of snares, tempter.

• **It can be frustrating,** when you have worried, scolded, and prayed every way you know to pray, and still the rebel does not surrender, the spiritually dead one does not come to life, the back-slider does not awake to revival.

• **It is neglected.** There is never enough time. Christian busyness often steals time from praying. We salute prayer like the flag, and use it little if at all. We normally do anything and everything else first. Prayer should be our first response, not the last resort.

• **But it is rewarding,** when in answer to prayer alone, God begins to break through in ways that are undeniably God.

In these days, prayer is not a nice add-on, an optional extra. It is your life. Isn't your family or another that you love in desperate enough straits to see that prayer is our only hope? My prayers begin before my feet hit the carpet in the bedroom each day. Before I make a cup of tea, I begin to greet God with praise, thanksgiving, and devotion. I plead the blood of Jesus and put on the armor. Then I am ready to seriously report to duty. Typically I pray **each day** the following prayers:

• **Praise** — lift up the names of God (**The I AM For Every Need,** p. 13, is one useful tool of the names and attributes of God).

• **Psalm 91** (p. 48) — This Psalm is mighty for proclaiming our provision under our covenant relationship with God.

• **Praying On The Armor** (p. 15) — Of all the pieces of the armor, putting on the belt of truth is foremost. If God's truth is not established in every thought, we will not use the power and provision of the other pieces.

• **Victory In Jesus** (p. 16) — I intentionally take my legal position under the blood of Jesus and in His atonement.

• **Warfare Prayer** (p. 17) — Spiritual warfare is primarily a truth encounter, not a power encounter. When we are grounded in truth, we have staying power to win the war for the family.

Then I spend some time wherever God leads in His Word, often in the Psalms and elsewhere, using the plan in **Renewing Your Mind,** p. 46. God nudges me toward promises, correction, commands, His character, and His ways. By commitment to the Word of God, I am renewing my mind in Him. Periodically as the need arises, I use the **Love Check-up** (p. 11), **Clean Hands Inventory** (p. 12), **Spirit Of Separation** (p. 24), or **Prayer Of Forgiveness** (p. 39) to keep short accounts with God. This is the way of continuous revival, which is letting God get me where He wants me to be, so that He can do what He wants to do.

After meditating in God's Word, I pray the following prayers out loud. They are more powerful to me as I pray aloud:

• **Bondage-Breaking Prayer** (p. 18) — When the battle is not against flesh and blood, only spiritual weapons are effective. The basis for this prayer is 1 Corinthians 10:3-5 and 2 Timothy 2:25-26. God will grant dramatic answers for those we love as we assail the gates of hell with this prayer.

• **Release From Generational Bondages** (p. 38) — This prayer is effectual to bring peace to households and family gatherings. Experientially, every family has these "Like father, like son" familiar issues. Scripturally, the basis for this is Exodus 20:5-6, Galatians 3:13-14, and many others.

• **Seven Blessings For Families** (p. 37) — This has become one of my two favorite bottom-line prayers to use when I am asked to pray for others. (The other one is **When You Don't Know What To Pray**, p. 45). It says it all. God will bless according to His perfect will. Intentionally speak blessings to others.

• **God Is Greater Declaration** (p. 41) — This is a faith-builder as I fix my focus on the truth of who God is.

• **Evening Prayer For The Home** (p. 47) — Ideally, this is read out loud at the close of the day by the head of your household.

• Several times a week, I pray **Praying For Your Husband** (p. 19) and **Praying For Children** (p. 33).

This is **what** I do. By now you are saying, "I can't do all that. This takes time!" What choice do we have? Aren't we desperate yet? What have we gained if we gain the whole world and lose our families? This is the reason **why** I do what I do — for the sake of my family and other families God has given me to pray for. People I know and love are defeated, desperately hurting, and in deception. We must come to the aid of the family under siege by an enemy that is playing for keeps with the future of our children and grandchildren.

Let's answer the question, "**How** do you find the time?" This must work for those who have to be on job by 7:30 and for the mom whose little ones awake before she does. Regardless of our stage of life, all of us are over-committed and have little discretionary time. I have put these prayers on 4x6 cards. One page easily fits on two cards. I pray them first thing in the morning and as needed. I carry them with me to pray in "odd moments" of time. I have recorded them on tape to pray while getting dressed or doing household chores, in the car, or while prayer-walking. Our minds are always actively thinking about something, most likely rehearsing problems and failures. While my body is busy, I re-program my mind with God's truth, praise, and intercession. With much use, I am hiding the principles in my heart for the Holy Spirit to recall in time of need. I have made tapes for my husband and our children to pray on the way to work or school. Be creative. Ask God how to make this practical for you. If you are desperate, you will make time to pray.

What are visible, provable results for the intercessor who prays this aggressively?

• **Hearing the voice of God** more clearly, cultivating intimacy of fellowship with Him, knowing Him and His heart and purposes.

• **Strength to stand in freedom** against the deceiver, setting the seal of the Spirit of truth over your heart and mind in hundreds of practical ways daily.

• **Standing in the battle for others**, to plead the fullness of God's promises, to press the full freedom Jesus died to give people who love the Lord, but who are now defeated, in pain, and deceived.

What are the minimum daily requirements to effectually use this *Praying For The Family* strategy?

• **Get alone with God** to know Him intimately. Do you really know Him, or do you just use Him? Be a knower, not a user. Set your body, soul, and spirit on His perspective. David said, "My heart is fixed, O God" *(Psa. 57:7)*. An established heart produces a stable life in a hectic world. Intimate communion with God must be priority before the pressures of the day. It must be done even by "night owls." Discipline yourself to go to bed earlier. The snooze button is not your friend. If you snooze, you lose.

• **Renew your mind** in the Word of God. Prayer is based on relationship, but it depends on fellowship, which can be disrupted or strained by ignorance, neglect, or insensitivity to the Spirit.

Our greatest need is to hear from Him, not recite to Him our clever opinions. Without waiting to know the Father's heart and will, our "prayers" may be no more than judgment or unsanctified sympathy. For my prayers to be purely God, I must hear from Him in His Word and pray His Word back to Him.

• **Be in unity with your authority.** I say to my husband, "Ask God, and His answer through you will be my answer." I have learned the hard way to be truly submitted to his will and better judgment. I am blessed when I stay under his covering. I invite enemy attack when I step outside. Being under authority is abiding in God's order. I receive the benefits of protection from temptation, safety, direction in life, standing in spiritual warfare, intimacy in the family of God, godly influence, encouragement, and protection from deception. Rejecting or actively opposing authority is rebellion, which reaps the consequences of forfeiting blessings, increasing sin, spiritual deafness, unteachability, distrust of God, enmity with God, vulnerability, God's judgment and discipline, to name only a few. We must have the humility and accountability of submission to God-given authority for survival. Our Father knows best.

• **Intercede for others and talk with God about your own "Give us this day our daily bread" issues.** Use **Steps to Powerful Prayer**, p. 9, as the basis for your intercession. The Holy Spirit is the Spirit of prayer. He inspires true intercession, not our own strength or understanding, as we present requests at the throne of God. By the Spirit, get the mind of Christ for a person or situation, and plead it with the Father, in Jesus' name. The wisest advice I can give is "Button it up and pray." Often people respond, "You mean just pray?" We are more willing to rely on our ability to scold, nag, convince, persuade, convict, preach, or modify behavior, as if it all depends on us. I get in God's way by such soulish tactics. God is in control! He has a plan! He is smart and loving! He does not need me to help Him by playing Holy Spirit. Allow the One who has all knowledge to work His will in His way and in His time in answer to your prayers. The One who redeemed and freed us will do the same for those we love.

• **Practice the presence of God.** Talk with our Father person-to-person, heart-to-heart. Consciously live life in His presence continuously and walk consistently with Him.

Steps To Powerful Prayer

1. **WORSHIP God** because He is an awesome God and worthy of our heart's affection and life's devotion. Reflect on His infinite greatness. "Enter into His gates with thanksgiving and His courts with praise" *(Psa. 100:4)*. Praise brings us into God's presence and forces Satan to flee. Praise is the most effectual but under-utilized power in the universe.

2. **BE STILL** and know that He is God *(Psa. 46:10)*. Quiet your heart before Him. Tell Him that you love Him.

3. **CONFESS** your sins and cover them with the blood of Jesus. Agree with God about your sins. Acknowledge that your sins have grieved His Spirit. Allow God to soften your heart and make you sensitive to His gentle correction. Repent and receive His forgiveness and cleansing. "If I regard iniquity in my heart, the Lord will not hear me *(Psa. 66.18)*. But if we confess our sins, He is faithful and just and will forgive us our sins and purify us from all unrighteousness" *(1 John 1:9)*.

4. **SUBMIT** to God with your whole being under His Lordship. "Humble yourselves, therefore, under God's mighty hand, that He may lift you up in due time" *(1 Pet. 5:6)*. Confess your position in Christ. Don't let the enemy rob you of who you are, what you have, and what you can do in Christ.

5. **BELIEVE** that God will hear and answer. "Without faith it is impossible to please God, because anyone who comes to Him must believe that He exists and that He rewards those who earnestly seek Him" *(Heb. 11:6)*.

6. **DO BATTLE** in spiritual warfare. "For our struggle is not against flesh and blood, but against the rulers, against the authorities, against the powers of this dark world and against the spiritual forces of evil in heavenly realms" *(Eph. 6:12)*. Recognize the power and strategy of the enemy, but be impressed that God is greater *(1 John 4:4)*! The atoning blood of Jesus has power to break the devil's dominion. Christ invested us with His delegated spiritual authority to bind the forces of darkness in His name *(Mat. 12:29)*. The devil has no legal power over us unless we concede ground to him.

He will give up to us only what he must. We will be fighting for contested ground, but the adversary must obey the blood of Jesus and His word of authority *(Eph. 2:6, Luke 10:19, Col. 2:15)*. We, as dear children, are from God and have overcome them, because the One who is in us is greater than the one who is in the world *(1 John 4:4)*.

7. **LISTEN** to the Holy Spirit. Prayer is more than asking. Learn to distinguish His voice. Be sensitive to His gentlest whisper. "No eye has seen, no ear has heard, no mind has conceived what God has prepared for those who love Him— but God has revealed it to us by His Spirit" *(1 Cor. 2:9-10)*.

8. **ASK GOD** what He wants you to pray about. Intercession is not reading God your shopping list. Remember He said, "I will do whatever you ask in My name, so that the Son may bring glory to the Father. You may ask Me for anything in My name, and I will do it" *(John 14:13-14)*.

9. **JOIN TOGETHER** in agreement with other believers. Ask God for a prayer partner who will pray with you as they pray for their family. "If two of you on earth agree about anything you ask for, it will be done for you by My Father in heaven. For where two or three come together in My name, there am I with them" *(Mat. 18:19-20)*.

10. **PERSIST** until the answer comes! "Keep on asking and it will be given you; keep on seeking and you will find; keep on knocking and the door will be opened to you" *(Mat. 7:7)*.

11. **PRAISE** the Lord that He has heard, and He will answer according to His will. "This is the confidence we have in approaching God: that if we ask anything according to His will, He hears us. And if we know that He hears us — whatever we ask— we know that we have what we asked of Him" *(1 John 5:14-15)*.

12. **ACT** on what God has revealed to you. Pray and obey. "Do whatever He tells you" *(John 2:5)*. Jesus gave a conditional promise, "If you abide in me and My words abide in you, you shall ask whatever you will and it shall be done unto you in My name" *(John 15:7)*. The promise is unlimited, but God's fulfilling it may depend on our abiding in truth *(2 Cor. 10:6)*.

Love Check-up

And now I will show you the most excellent way.
~ 1 Corinthians 12:31b ~

"Let no debt remain outstanding, except the continuing debt to love one another" *(Rom. 13:8).* Prepare your heart for praying for your family. Let God search your heart toward them with this love check-up. Love deficit hinders effective prayer, because you are not free to have the mind of Christ who loved all people enough to die for them. Faith without love is not effectual, because faith works through love *(1 Cor. 13:2, Gal. 5:6).*

Lord, make 1 Corinthians 13:4-7 live in me!

❏ ♥ Love endures long and is slow to lose patience.
❏ ♥ Love is kind.
❏ ♥ Love does not envy and is not jealous.
❏ ♥ Love does not boast and is not anxious to impress.
❏ ♥ Love is not proud or arrogant.
❏ ♥ Love has good manners and is not rude.
❏ ♥ Love does not gratify self nor insist on its own way.
❏ ♥ Love is not touchy or easily angered.
❏ ♥ Love keeps no record of wrongs.
❏ ♥ Love never delights in evil.
❏ ♥ Love rejoices with the truth.
❏ ♥ Love has no limit to its endurance.
❏ ♥ Love always trusts and is ready to believe the best.
❏ ♥ Love never loses hope.
❏ ♥ Love always perseveres and can outlast anything.
❏ ♥ Love never fails nor comes to an end.

Are you loving your family as Jesus does? If not, confess it as sin, repent, and receive God's forgiveness and grace *(1 John 1:9).* The Father's love is our source *(1 John 3:1).* Jesus is our model *(John 15:13).* The Holy Spirit makes it real *(Rom. 5:5).*

Now these three things remain: faith, hope, and love.
But the greatest of these is love *(1 Cor. 13:13).*

Clean Hands, Pure Heart Inventory

Jesus told His disciples, "The prince of this world is coming and he has nothing in Me" *(John 14:30)*. To get on victory ground to pray for your family, take some time to prayerfully ask, "Father, in Jesus' name, show me areas where I need to take back ground that I have conceded to Satan. Identify for me my key issues. I submit to You, resist the devil, and he must flee. By Your Spirit, I covenant to keep a clean slate with You every day."

Make a list of each of the following:

1. Involvement in the occult, cults, and false religions.
2. Lies you have believed (fear of failure, rejection, punishment, etc.), defense mechanisms (denial, withdrawal, blame, shame, etc.), fears, painful memories or emotions that won't go away.
3. Unforgiveness that has festered around areas of woundedness (abandonment, rejection, shame, fear of failure, punishment). List people who have wronged or hurt you. (These prompters insure your honesty — "I resent ..." "I need to forgive ...").
4. Evidences of rebellion (Remember that rebellion is as the sin of witchcraft) — people/institutions you have been rebellious toward, incidences or patterns of personal willfulness.
5. Evidences of areas of pride in your life. Arrogance or stubbornness is as idolatry *(1 Sam. 15:23)*.
6. Ties that bind — list everybody with whom you have been sexually involved, list friends that have strongly influenced you unrighteously and specify how, list a way of life you are tied to (people-pleasing, location, social set, occupational environment, etc.), list addictions, vows, inner vows ("I will never ..."). These compete with allegiance to God only.
7. Generational bondages — list major unrighteous character traits of close relatives (living and dead), curses operative in your family line, secret organizations to which you or your relatives have sworn an oath.

Pray this way, **"Father, I renounce these strongholds of the enemy. I plead the blood of Jesus over each of these. I renounce my sin, resist the enemy, and submit to You to be filled with Your righteousness in these areas."**

This is vital to your victory in Jesus and your position of intercession for your family.

The I AM . . . For Our Every Need

Sooner or later, everyone will be beat up, battered, bruised, and burned out by the daily issues of life. Good news! God is Lord of all of your life. List every need and emotion that you are feeling, no matter how inconsequential they seem. After you have acknowledged all your emotions and needs, go through the names of God until you find the expression of His character that meets each need. For every need, there is a corresponding attribute of God. Affirm that God is still God, no matter how you feel. Have a praise party, not a pity-party, for your loving Father is a big God. He is able to do much more than you need or can think or ask.

He is . . . . for our needs

Abba Father...when we need fathering
Acceptance...when we feel unwanted
Adequacy..for our inadequacy
All-sufficient..in our hardest situations
Amen...............................when we need Him to be the last Word
Answer.......................................for our uncertainty and questions
Author of faith.............................for our unbelief or doubt
Bread of life...for our spiritual hunger
Bridegroom...................when we need companionship and cherishing
Broken and spilled out for us........................when we've been used
Burden bearer...when we are heavy laden
Before all things...when we're surprised
Cleansing...for our defilement and shame
Closer than a brother....................................when we are lonely
Comforter who wipes away tears.........in our griefs and sorrows
Defender..when we are under attack
Deliverer, liberty....................................for our bondage or captivity
Door......................................when it looks as if there's no way out
Sure foundation.........................when we're shaking and insecure
Faithful friend..when friends fail us
Fullness..when we're empty
God of details..when we're frustrated
God of love..........................when we feel unloved and need a hug
God who is there ....when we feel alone or abandoned
Guide and way...................when we're confused and need direction

Grace...................when we're too hard on ourselves or others
Healer...............for woundedness, rejection, physical sickness
Hope.......................when we are discouraged and want to quit
Humility..for our pride
Joy...when we are depressed
Keeper and Protector...........................when we are vulnerable
Lifter of our head...........................when we feel oppressed
Long-suffering, slow to anger.....when we have blown it again
Mercy...for criticism and unkindness
Mighty God, our strength.........for our weakness or temptation
Never-failing, the same...........when we are fickle and faithless
Overcoming victory...........................for defeat and depression
Prince of peace...when we are stressed, worried, and confused
Provider...for every financial need
Quieter of the storm................for struggles without and within
Reconciliation...............................for breaches in relationships
Rest...when we're tired and can't go on
Restorer of our soul........when we're bruised and beaten down
Reviver, living water.........when we are depleted, barren, thirsty
Satisfaction ....when we've tried everything
Song, praise..................when we're joyless and heavy of heart
Spirit of the Lord...............................when we need to be set free
Strong..when we're weak
Trinity unity...for mending separation
Truth...in spite of what the world says
True riches...........................when we covet the world's wealth
Vindicator ....when we have been wronged
Way-maker...........................when a solution seems impossible
Wisdom...for our hard choices

This is just a beginning. Make your own alphabet of the names and character of God as a personal affirmation that He is more than adequate as your Need-meeter. God is a covenant-keeping God. He is covenantally committed to being true to His names and attributes by which He has revealed Himself to His people. He is enthroned in your situation and life as you call His names *(1 Chron. 13:6)*.

Gaze at God, glance at the need, and entrust it to His all-wise, all-loving care. He is the Lord, the Most High God who reigns over all. To whom else would we go? He alone is the Word of eternal life *(John 6:68)*. **Glory!**

Praying on the Armor

The Word of God commands us to be strong in the Lord and in His mighty power *(Eph. 6:10-18)*. We must daily stand firm against the devil's schemes by putting on our spiritual armor. It is as important to dress spiritually each day as it is to dress physically. Therefore, declare daily that you are obeying God's command to stand in all the armor available to intercessory soldiers in the battle for our families.

Father, our struggle is not against flesh and blood, but against the rulers, the authorities, the powers of this dark world and the spiritual forces of evil in the heavenly realms. They are merely fallen angels cast down from heaven by the command of the true and living God. They are in subjection to Jesus Christ, the Son of God. We are in Him and stand in His already-assured victory. Therefore, we put on the full armor of God, so that when the fiery darts come, we may be able to stand our ground.

We stand firm because we have taken up these weapons:
• We buckle the belt of truth around our waist— Truth is the Person of our Lord Jesus. He is the way, the truth, and the life.
• We put on the breastplate of righteousness — The Person and sinless sacrifice of the Lord Jesus Christ is our Righteousness.
• We put on our feet the sandals of preparation of the gospel of peace— The person of the Lord Jesus Christ Himself is our peace.
 • We take the shield of faith which extinguishes all the flaming arrows of the evil one— The Person of the Lord Jesus Christ is the Author and Finisher of our faith. He is all the faith we need.
• We take the helmet of salvation— My Lord Jesus Christ Himself alone is my salvation. His mind guards our minds.
• We take the sword of the Spirit, which is the Word of God — The Word is the Person of Jesus who came in the flesh and defeated the works of the enemy. His Word never returns void.
• We clothe ourselves in all of Jesus and pray in the Spirit on all occasions with all kinds of prayers and requests.

"No weapon formed against us will prevail, and we will refute every tongue that accuses us. This is the heritage of the servants of the Lord, and this is their vindication from Me," declares the Lord *(Isa. 54:17)*. The One who was born of God keeps us safe, and the evil one cannot harm us *(1 John 5:18)*. In Jesus' name, Amen.

Victory In Jesus

You are the Name above all names, the Lord of heaven and earth, King of all kings, El Elyon-Most High God, Captain of the Lord's hosts. You are the Commander of all commanders, the Commander of the armies of heaven who has no equal who cannot lose, and You are by our side.

All power is yours, Sovereign God our Father. We confess Jesus as our Savior and Lord. We are in Christ, redeemed by His sacrifice on the cross, cleansed, and clothed in His righteousness. We do not presume our safety. We step intentionally into the protection of the blood of the worthy Lamb of God. We plead the mighty name of our Lord Jesus Christ over all our personal lives, all our family, all possessions, our jobs and businesses, our ministries, and the people in our personal and spiritual jurisdiction. The blood of the spotless Lamb of God is our Shield of protection from the destructive intent of the enemy. Jesus has given us legitimate authority to tread on all the power of the enemy, and nothing shall injure us *(Luke 10:19)*.

Because of the cross of Jesus, the devil has no place in us, no power, dominion, or authority over us. We overcome him by the victory of the blood of Jesus. He has no unsettled claims nor effectual assignments against us. We stand against every lie the deceiver ever told us. We take back all ground we ever gave him and close every door we ever opened to him, intentionally or in ignorance. We refuse his accusations and condemnation, because all our sins and guilt are nailed to the cross. We refuse to converse with the devil. We refuse his tactics of fear and intimidation. Our weapons through God are mighty to pull down enemy strongholds. In the name of Jesus, in His authority, by His blood, according to His Word, and in the power of His Spirit, we pull down every stronghold of the enemy in our lives. We resist everything that exalts itself against knowing God and obeying His will.

We overcome the enemy by the blood of the Lamb and by the word of our testimony. We claim the perfect freedom of Jesus. We receive all the fullness the Holy Spirit living in us. We yield all of ourselves to all of God. We plead, Thy kingdom come, Thy will be done, in our lives as it is in heaven this day. We stand in all the victory that is in Christ Jesus, in whose precious name we pray, Amen.

Warfare Prayer

Father, I bow in worship, praise, and thanksgiving before You. I surrender myself completely to You. I am covered with the blood of the Lord Jesus Christ as my protection. I am submitted to God, I resist the devil, and he must flee. In the name of Jesus, I bring the blood of the Lamb against all the works of the enemy.

True and living God, You are worthy to receive all glory and honor. You love me; You sent Your Son to die as my substitute; You completely forgave me through Him; You gave me His perfect righteousness; You made me complete in Him; He won total victory for me on the cross and in His resurrection; You adopted me into Your family; You assumed all responsibility for me; You offer Yourself to me to be my daily help and strength. Your provision for me is complete. Blessed Holy Spirit, I live and pray this day in complete dependence on You. Pray Your prayers through me.

I have mighty spiritual weapons. I choose to stand aggressively in the full armor which is Jesus Himself. I claim all His victory today. I am now seated in heaven with Him. In Jesus' name, the enemy is under my feet. In Jesus' name, I tear down the strongholds of Satan and reject all his plans formed against my body, mind, will, and emotions. I reject all his schemes of hindrance, insinuation, accusation, temptation, lies, and deception. Show me where I am giving any ground to him, and cleanse me from every foothold.

The Word of God is true, and I will obey You and abide in You. I put off the works of the old man, and I stand in the victory of Jesus to cleanse me from the flesh and enable me to live above sin. I put off all _____ (my greatest struggles—selfishness, fear, doubt, lust, etc.) and put on _____ (the new nature of holiness, righteousness, truth, courage, strength, faith, etc.).

You blessed me with all spiritual blessings in Christ Jesus. I welcome the Holy Spirit living in me to fulfill Your will. Transform me and fill me with Your love, joy, peace, patience, kindness, goodness, faithfulness, gentleness, and self-control.

I stand on victory ground for today. I claim all the work of the cross of Jesus, His resurrection power, His ascended authority, and Pentecost for all my victory. You are Lord of all my life this day. In Jesus' name, Amen.

Adapted from Warfare Prayer by Dr. Victor Matthews.

Bondage Breaking Prayer

Father, we come boldly to Your throne of grace, and find mercy and grace to help in time of need. Grant _____ release from bondage to strongholds of the enemy. We plead the blood of Jesus to cancel all commands of the powers of darkness in _____'s life. Jesus came to destroy the works of the devil. His blood defeated the god of this age. In Jesus' name, take back all ground _____ gave the enemy. Draw _____ out of bondage and deception.

We have the heavenly intercession of the Holy Spirit and Jesus. Father, focus the intercession of the Spirit on _____. Answer these prayers according to Your perfect will. Lord Jesus, our Intercessor, apply all Your mighty work against the enemy. Bring all the power of the incarnation, crucifixion, resurrection, and ascension against the assignments seeking to destroy _____. Most High God, contend with those who contend with _____. Rebuke the enemy in all his operations. Dispatch mighty warrior angels to do battle on _____'s behalf.

Send Your light and Your truth and lead ____. Remove all spiritual blindness, deafness, and hardness of heart. Grant _____ eyes to see, ears to hear, and a heart that seeks You. I plead Your mercy and grace over all _____'s personal sin, failure, and family iniquities. Break through and heal _____'s wounded spirit. Bind a hedge of thorns around ____ that will repel all the works of darkness in _____'s life.

This battle is not against flesh and blood, and we have spiritual weapons that set captives free. By Your Holy Spirit, break every yoke of bondage in _____'s life. Grant _____ conviction of sin with godly sorrow to repentance and deliverance from captivity. Set _____ completely free. It is written, you shall know the truth and the Truth shall set you free. We overcome by the blood of the Lamb and by the word of our testimony. Thank You for Your mighty work by the blood of Christ Jesus. Thank You for granting me the grace, power, persistence, and love in intercession with faith for _____ until You are glorified in their life. In Jesus' name, Amen.

Adapted and abridged from "The Adversary" by Mark Bubeck, who has also written other mighty doctrinal prayers.

Praying For Your Husband

May the God of peace Himself make my husband entirely pure and devoted to God; and may His spirit, soul, and body be kept strong and blameless until that day when our Lord Jesus Christ comes back again (1 Thes. 5:23).

These Scripture-based prayers will challenge you and help you in your most important duty as a wife— *praying for your husband.* Because you are one flesh with him, no one else stands in as strong a position in your prayers for him as you do. Make your husband your daily prayer priority. Pray diligently every day for him. Plead for God's mercy on him. Give thanks for all God is going to do for him *(1 Tim. 2:1).*

As you read your Bible, claim other promises and pray other truths into his life. Using the Word of God, pray for him from the top of his head to the soles of his feet. Present every part of his body to God *(Rom. 6:11-14).*

His Head

Lord, Thank You for giving me my husband. You are his head *(1 Cor. 11:3).* Help me allow him to be my head, as Christ is head of the church *(Eph. 5:23).* Thank You for being head over all and for Your perfect plans for our home.

**The closer we are to Jesus,
the closer we will be to each other.**

His Mind

Lord, I pray that my husband will have the rich experience of knowing Christ with real certainty and clear understanding. Your plan for him is Christ Himself, and in Him are contained all the treasures of wisdom and knowledge *(Col. 2:2-3).* May he not be fleshly minded but spiritually minded which is life and peace *(Rom. 8:6).* Capture all his thoughts to obey Christ *(2 Cor. 10:5).*

I pray that he will receive what Christ is teaching him and let His words enrich his life and make him wise *(Col. 3:16).* Fill his thoughts with You so he doesn't spend so much time worrying about earthly things *(Col. 3:2).* Fix his thoughts on what is true, good, right, lovely, and positive. Remind him to think about all he has to praise you for and be glad about *(Phi. 4:8).*

Thank You that You open his mind to understand the scriptures *(Luke 24:45)*. I pray that he will not be conformed to this world but be transformed by renewing his mind in Your Word, so that he may experience Your good, acceptable, and perfect will *(Rom. 12:2)*.

His Eyes

Open his eyes that he may truly see from Your perspective *(2 Kings 6:17)*. May he keep his eyes alert for spiritual danger, stand strong and true to You, and be Your man *(1 Cor. 16:13)*. Help him to watch for the snares of Satan, our enemy *(1 Pet. 5:8)*.

I pray that he will keep looking steadily into Your law for free men, so that he does what it says, so that You may greatly bless him in everything he does *(Jam. 1:25)*. Make him always discern the difference between right and wrong and be inwardly clean so that no one can find fault in him *(Phi. 1:10)*. Give him wisdom to see clearly and really understand who Christ is and all that He did for him. Flood his heart with Your light so that he can see the future You have called us to share *(Eph. 1:17-18)*.

His Ears

Father, Your Word says that faith comes by hearing and hearing by Your Word *(Rom. 10:17)*. I pray that my husband will hear Your words with His heart, not just his head *(Psa. 78:1)*. Cause him to hear Your voice as You instruct him *(Deu. 4:36)*.

Speak to him again and again. Open his ears and give him wisdom, causing him to know Your mind, keeping him from pride, warning him of the penalties of sin, and keeping him from Satan's temptations *(Job 33:14-17)*. When You speak to him, I pray that he will listen and not resist *(Isa. 50:5)*.

His Nose

Thank you, Lord, the sweet, wholesome fragrance of You fills his life. It is Your presence within him, an aroma of Jesus to both the saved and the unsaved around him. May my husband's life be refreshing to others, a life-giving perfume *(2 Cor. 2:15)*.

His Mouth

Set a watch, O Lord, over his mouth and keep the door of his lips *(Psa. 141:3)*. Grant to him great boldness in testimony *(Acts 4:29)*. Give him Your words so that he may boldly make

Jesus known *(Eph. 6:19)*. Give him many chances to share the Good News of Christ and help him tell it lovingly, freely, fully, and plainly. Help him to make the most of his opportunities to tell others about victory in Jesus and to be wise in all his contacts. Let his conversation be gracious and wise, for then he will have the right answer for everyone *(Col. 4:3-6)*. Give him Your words so that he may know what to say to all *(Isa. 50:4)*. Whatever he does or says, let it be as a representative of the Lord Jesus *(Col. 3:17)*.

Help him not to complain or argue in all that he does *(Phi. 2:14)*. Sweeten his words to say only what is good and helpful and what will bless others *(Eph. 4:29)*. Cause him to abstain from dirty stories, unholy talk, and coarse jokes *(Eph. 5:4)*.

I pray that we will talk to each other much about You, quoting psalms and hymns and singing songs, making music in our hearts to You *(Eph. 5:19)*. Let the words of his mouth and the meditation of his heart be acceptable to You *(Psa. 19:14)*.

His Bones

Bring health to his body and nourishment to his bones as he fears You, rejects evil, and keeps himself from bitterness *(Job 21:23-25, Pro. 3:7-8)*. Guide him continually, Lord, and satisfy his soul in drought and strengthen him, so that he will be like a watered garden, a spring of water which does not fail *(Isa. 58:11)*.

His Heart

Dear Father, please enable my husband to obey Your command to love You with all his heart, with all his soul, and with all his might *(Deu. 6:5)*. Let his heart be filled with You alone to make him pure and true *(Jam. 4:8)*.

Thank You for Your promise: "A new heart I will give him, and a new spirit I will put within him; and I will take away the stony heart from him and will give him a heart of flesh. I will put My Spirit within him and cause him to walk in my statutes, and he will keep My judgments and do them" *(Eze. 36:26-27)*. You desire to make his heart soft *(Job 23:16)*. Create in him a clean heart filled with pure thoughts and right desires *(Psa. 51:10)*. Warn him not to harden his heart *(Psa. 95:8)*. Help him to keep his heart with all diligence *(Pro. 4:23)*, because whatever is in his heart overflows into his speech *(Luke 6:45)*.

May he be transformed in his heart in the fear of the Lord every day. Cause him to trust in You, Lord, with all his heart and lean not unto his own understanding *(Pro. 3:5)*. May he worship You and serve You with a clean heart and a willing mind, for You see his heart and know his every thought *(1 Chron. 28:9)*.

I pray that he will let the peace of God rule his heart *(Col. 3:15)*. I pray that Christ will be more at home in his heart, as he trusts You more fully. May his roots go down deep into Your marvelous love. May he be able to feel and understand how long, how wide, how deep, and how high your love is and to experience this love for himself, although it is so great that he will never reach the end of it. Fill him up with You, God *(Eph. 3:17-19)*.

His Arms

Be gracious to my husband, as he waits for You. Be His arm every morning and His salvation in the time of trouble *(Isa. 33:2)*. Remind him that You say, "The man who trusts in man, who relies on the flesh, and whose heart departs from the Lord is cursed. The man who trusts in the Lord and whose hope is the Lord is blessed" *(Jer. 17:5, 7)*.

His Hands

I pray, Lord, that he will continue to bless You as long as he lives, lifting up his hands to You in prayer *(Psa. 63:4)*. You want men everywhere to pray with holy hands lifted to You, free from sin, anger, and resentment *(1 Tim. 2:8)*.

His Legs

Thank You, Lord, that my husband will walk by faith and not by sight, as he looks to You *(2 Cor. 5:7)*. May he use every piece of Your armor to resist the enemy whenever he attacks, so that he will stand firm *(Eph. 6:13)*. Help him lay aside every weight and the sins that seek to make him fall, so he can run with patience the race that You have set before him *(Heb. 12:1)*.

His Feet

Thank you, Lord, for keeping him from discouragement and for setting his feet on a firm path. Continue to steady him as he walks along *(Psa. 40:2)*. Hold his feet to Your path *(Psa. 66:9)*. The steps of a good man are directed by You. Thank You that You delight in each step that he takes *(Psa. 37:23)*. Thank You for giving him power to tread on serpents and scorpions and over all the power of the enemy *(Luke 10:19)*.

A Prayer For Our Marriage

Help us to walk together in the light of Jesus, so we can have true fellowship of spirit with each other *(1 John 1:7)*. Enable us to honor You by submitting to each other *(Eph. 5:21)*. Help us to live in complete harmony with the attitude of Christ toward each other *(Rom. 15:5)*, as You give patience, faithfulness, and encouragement. May we live joyfully in Your love through all the days of life *(Ecc. 9:9)*. May he be faithful and true to me, rejoicing in the wife of his youth. May my tender embrace satisfy him. May my love alone fill him with delight *(Pro. 5:15, 18, 19)*. A good wife is worth more than precious gems. Let him know that he can trust me and that I am dedicated to helping him all my days *(Pro. 31:10-12)*.

I will not get weary in prayer but keep praying and watching for Your answers. I will thank You when they come *(Col. 4:2)*. I will keep on rejoicing in You, for I know that as I pray for my husband, and the Holy Spirit helps him, everything works for our good and Your glory *(Phi. 1:19, Rom. 8:28-29)*.

By Your mighty power at work in my husband and me, You are able to do far more than I could ask or even dream— beyond my highest prayers, desires, hopes, or thoughts. I praise You and give You glory *(Eph. 3:20-21)*. Amen.

The original prayer for husbands is attributed to Connie VandePol, Bowling Green, KY.

"Let the wife see that she respects and reverences her husband — that she notices him, regards him, honors him, prefers him, venerates and esteems him; and that she defers to him, praises him, and loves and admires him exceedingly."
(*Eph. 5:33* Amplified)
Ask your husband, "How am I doing?"

Spirit Of Separation

Every kingdom divided against itself will be ruined,
and every city or household divided against itself will not stand.
~ Matthew 12:25 ~

How timely is the picture of separation in the last days, "But mark this: There will be terrible times in the last days. People will be lovers of themselves, lovers of money, boastful, proud, abusive, disobedient to their parents, ungrateful, unholy, without love, unforgiving, slanderous, without self-control, brutal, not lovers of the good, treacherous, rash, conceited, lovers of pleasure rather than lovers of God – having a form of godliness but denying its power. Have nothing to do with them" *(2 Tim. 3:1-5)*.

Why is the spirit of separation so serious? Spiritual authority is present in proportion to the unity of relationships among believers moving toward a common God-given goal. Therefore, separation is Satan's foundational tool to divide and conquer. His first act toward man was to separate him from God in the Garden of Eden.

The spirit of separation works in marriages, friendships, families, churches, denominations, groups, between races, at the office, at school, between nations – wherever there are people!

Practical remedy for separation— prayer application

1. Recognize how the spirit of separation operates.

2. Renounce its operation in you. Repent of your sins of separation one by one. Let the blood of Jesus cover them all. The power in this prayer application depends on your own repentance of separation at work in you *(Mat. 7:1-5)*.

3. Don't try in your own flesh to dismantle the walls of separation of others *(Gal. 5:15, 1 Tim. 4:16, 2 Cor. 13:5)*. This is a spiritual battle, not one against flesh and blood *(2 Cor. 10:3-6, Eph. 6:12)*.

4. As you pray to uproot each of the workings of the spirit of separation, pray to plant or establish the opposite spirit, which

is the work or nature of Jesus for each one. In the box below, these opposites are in bold beside each of the twenty manifestations of the spirit of separation. Pray this way: "I repent of **pride**, and renounce its control in my life. Father, work in me the spirit of **humility**, as you fill me with the fullness of the sweet Spirit of Christ Jesus. I repent of **self-centeredness** ..."

Spirit of separation	vs.	God's spirit
1. **Pride** (vanity, arrogance)		**Humility**
2. **Self-centeredness** (jealousy, rivalry)		**Sacrifice**
3. **Deception** (vain imaginations, idolatry)		**Truth**
4. **No fear of God** (rebellion, disobedience)		**Fear of the Lord**
5. **Control** (manipulation, occult)		**Filling of the Spirit**
6. **Rejection** (insecurity)		**Acceptance**
7. **Accusation** (judging, criticism, mocking)		**Grace**
8. **Unforgiveness** (resentment, bitterness)		**Forgiveness**
9. **Sins of the fathers** (including curses)		**The cross**
10. **Perversion of God-intended roles**		**Submission**
11. **Confusion** (disorder)		**Godly wisdom**
12. **Apathy** (not caring)		**Love**
13. **Ignorance**		**Mercy and truth**
14. **Busyness**		**Waiting on God**
15. **Lust** (coveting)		**Holiness**
16. **Materialism** (greed, worldliness)		**Extravagant Generosity**
17. **Withdrawal**		**Trinity unity**
18. **Anger** (hatred, violence, provocation)		**Death-to-self**
19. **Racism** (prejudice)		**Reconciliation and restoration**
20. **Death**		**Life**

5. Pray for God to send His Spirit to overcome and restore. Ask God to establish the kingdom rule of His Lordship in relationships and in the body of Christ. Sow restoration by His next steps of obedience: praise, prayer, repentance, restitution, confirming your love; affirmation, faith, rejoicing, endurance, etc., as God leads.

The ultimate cure for separation is union in the Head *(Eph. 4:1-16)*, abiding in the Vine *(John 15:1-16)*, oneness in the family *(John 17, 1 John 5:1)*, and fellowship in the Spirit *(Phi. 2:1-5)*.

Praying For Your Wife

These personalized scripture prayers will challenge you in your most important duty as a husband—praying for your wife. Your prayers provide a covering of grace and protection for her. Make this commitment, "Far be it from me that I should sin against the Lord by failing to pray for my wife *(1 Sam. 12:23)*. I affirm my responsibility of loving, covenant-keeping headship of my wife. I am the head of my wife as Christ is the head of the church, His body, of which He is the Savior *(Eph. 5:23)*. My head is Christ, and the head of Christ is God *(1 Cor. 11:3)*. Lord, help me to be her loving head as You are mine, according to Your perfect plan. Thank You for being Lord over all in our home."

Read these Scripture verses from your Bible at least once to "glean" all God might have for you to pray. As you read your Bible devotionally, mark other Scripture promises to claim and other truths to pray into her life.

Every day, pray for her from the top of her head to the soles of her feet using the Word of God. Present every part of her body to God, as His vessel of righteousness and grace *(Rom. 6:13-14)*.

It's your job to love her and cherish her.
It's God's job to make her a loving wife.

Her Spirit

Father, because Jesus is her Savior and Lord, You have put Your Holy Spirit in my wife *(Eze. 36:26-27, Rom. 8:9-11,16)*. By Your gracious Spirit within her, grow in her life Your abundant fruit — love, joy, peace, patience, kindness, goodness, faithfulness, gentleness and self-control *(Gal. 5:22-23)*, as she dedicates herself to being filled daily with Your Spirit.

Her Mind

Lord, open her mind to see You in Your Word and to receive Your truth *(Luke 24:45)*. By Your work in her, she is made new in the attitude of her mind. I pray that she will choose to put on the new self, created to be like You in righteousness and holiness *(Eph. 4:23-24)*. I pray that she will not be conformed to the world, but be transformed by renewing her mind in Your Word, so that she can discern and accept Your perfect will *(Rom. 12:2)*.

I pray that my wife will personally know You as her Lord with certainty and devotion. May she seek You alone, the source of all wisdom *(Col. 2:2-3)*. May she make it a priority to grow in being intimately acquainted with You and all Your ways *(Phi. 3:8-10)*. May she obey You with all her thoughts *(2 Cor. 10:5)*. May she not set her mind on worldly things, but ask Your Spirit to control her thoughts, which is life and peace *(Rom. 8:6, 9)*.

I pray that she will think on Your truth, and let Your words enrich her life *(Col. 3:16)*. Fix her mind on heaven's perspective, so she does not worry about things on earth *(Col. 3:1-3)*. Cause her thoughts to dwell on what is true, good, right, pure, lovely, and admirable in her circumstances and in others. Remind her to think about everything she has to praise You for in all things *(Phi. 4:8)*.

Her Eyes

Keep her eyes firmly fixed on You, Lord *(Heb. 12:2)*. Open her eyes to see spiritual truth *(Psa. 119:18, 2 Kings 6:17)*. You are the Way, the Truth, and the Life *(John 14:6)*.

May she keep her eyes open for spiritual danger, be spiritually alert, stand firm in the faith, and be courageous and strong *(1 Cor. 16:13)*. Help her to watch out for sly attacks from the enemy *(1 Pet. 5:8)*. Keep her desiring and expecting to see Your presence in her life continuously *(2 Cor. 11:3)*. Keep her looking into Your perfect Word that gives freedom, doing what she reads there, so that You may bless her *(Jam. 1:25)*. May she clearly discern what is best, so that she may be pure and blameless *(Phi. 1:9-11)*. Grant her the Spirit of wisdom and revelation to enlighten her heart, so that she may know You better, understand Your glorious inheritance in her, and experience Your great power daily in practical ways *(Eph. 1:17-19)*.

Her Ears

Father, faith comes by hearing, and hearing comes by Your Word *(Rom. 10:17)*. I pray that my wife will receive Your instruction *(Psa. 78:1)*. May she be sensitive to Your gentlest whisper of guidance *(Isa. 30:21)*. Awaken her each morning to listen You. As You speak to her, I pray she will not be rebellious or draw back from following You fully *(Isa. 50:4-5)*. May she receive your discipline *(Deu. 4:36)* to warn her of the price of sin, to turn her from wrong, and to keep her from pride *(Job 33:17)*.

Her Mouth

Let her words and her thoughts be pleasing in Your sight *(Psa. 19:14)*. Give her Your words so that she may know how to encourage weary or misguided ones *(Isa. 50:4)*. Open her mouth in godly wisdom and faithful instruction *(Pro. 31:26)*.

Grant her boldness for You *(Acts 4:29, Eph. 6:19)*. Open many doors for her to share the good news of Jesus freely, fully, and clearly. May she make the most of every opportunity as Your ambassador *(2 Cor. 5:20)*. May she answer everyone with gracious words *(Col. 4:3-6)*. Whatever she does or says, let it be an expression of the love, grace, and humility of Jesus *(Col. 3:17)*.

Help her to stay her heart on You, so that she will not complain or argue *(Phi. 2:14)*. Set a guard over her mouth *(Psa. 141:3)*. Remind her not to say hurtful or judgmental things about others, but to say only what is wholesome and helpful for building others up according to their needs *(Eph. 4:29)*. I pray that we will talk to each other much about You, quoting psalms, singing songs, making music in our hearts to You *(Eph. 5:19)*.

Her Bones

May my wife not be wise in her own eyes, but fear the Lord and shun evil. This will bring health to her body and nourishment to her bones *(Pro. 3:7-8)*. Strengthen her body, so that she will be like a well-watered garden, an unfailing spring *(Isa. 58:11)*.

Her Heart

May my wife worship You with wholehearted devotion and a willing spirit, for You, Lord, search the heart and understand every motive *(1 Chron. 18:9)*. Enable her to obey Your command to love You with all her heart, all her soul, all her strength, and all her mind *(Luke 10:27)*. Draw her close to Your heart, so that You alone will fill her heart to make her pure and true *(Jam. 4:8)*.

Thank You for Your promise: "I will give you a new heart. I will remove your heart of stone and give you a heart of flesh. And I will put my Spirit in you and cause you to follow my decrees and be careful to keep my laws" *(Eze. 36:26-27)*. Create in my wife that new, clean heart filled with pure thoughts and right desires *(Psa. 51:10)*. You desire her to have a teachable heart, so warn her not to harden her heart toward You *(Psa. 95:7-8)*.

Help her to guard her heart with all diligence, for it is the wellspring of life *(Pro. 4:23)*. Cause her to speak good words from Your goodness stored up in her heart. Empower Your goodness in her heart to overflow to others continually and in increasing measure *(Luke 6:45)*.

I pray she will trust in You, Lord, with all her heart, to acknowledge You in all her ways, and not to lean on her own understanding. Thereby You promise to direct her in wise choices *(Pro. 3:5-6)*. I pray that she will let Your peace rule her heart as Your Word dwells in her. By the example of her confidence in You, may she teach others with all wisdom and gratitude *(Col. 3:15-16)*. I pray that Christ will be more and more at home in her heart as she trusts in You. May her foundation be established deep in Your marvelous love. Enable her to understand and experience how wide and long and high and deep Your love really is, although it is so great we can never get to the end of it, so that she may be filled up with all the fullness of God *(Eph. 3:17-19)*. See to it that no root of bitterness grows in her heart and causes trouble in her relationships *(Heb. 12:15)*.

Her Arms

Make her arms strong for the tasks You give her *(Pro. 31:17)*. Cause her to look to You for her strength every morning and her salvation in time of distress *(Isa. 33:2)*. Remind her that you say, "The one who trusts in man, who depends on flesh for his strength, is cursed. He will dwell in the parched places of the desert. But the one who trusts in the Lord, whose confidence is in Him, is blessed. He will be like a tree planted by the water. It does not fear when heat comes; its leaves are always green. It has no worries in a year of drought and never fails to bear fruit" *(Jer. 17:5-8)*. May she trust in You alone and never fail to bear fruit in every good work, drawing from Your eternal fruitfulness *(Col. 1:10)*. Arm her with strength for Your spiritual battles and make her way perfect as she obeys You *(Psa. 18:32,39)*.

Her Hands

I pray that she will continue to bless You as long as she lives, lifting up her hands to You in prayer *(Psa. 63:4)*. As You direct her, may she open her hands to the needy *(Pro. 31:20)*. Train her hands for warfare, obeying You as her Commander *(Psa. 18:34)*. Cause her to be a strong soldier of the cross in the grace of

Christ Jesus, and keep her from entanglements that would hinder her from pleasing You *(2 Tim. 2:1,3-4)*.

Her Legs

May she use all Your armor to resist the enemy when he attacks, so that she may stand strong in You *(Eph. 6:10-13)*. Help her to lay aside every weight and the sins that would cause her to fall, so that she can run with patience the race that You have set before her *(Heb. 12:1)*. Teach her to recognize godly counsel and not follow ungodly advice. Cause her to delight in Your truth, knowing that You promise to watch over the way of the righteous *(Psa. 1:1-2, 6)*.

Her Feet

Help her to walk by faith, and not by sight *(2 Cor. 5:7)*. Teach her to hope in You, as You promised in Isaiah 40:31— "Those who wait on the Lord will renew their strength. They will soar on wings like eagles; they will run and not grow weary, they will walk and not be faint."

I pray that her walk with You in Your wisdom and understanding will glorify You. May she walk worthy of Your name and please You in every way, growing in knowing You, being strengthened in Your power, so that she may have great endurance, patience, joy, and gratitude *(Col. 1:9-12)*.

Thank You for lifting her out of discouragement when things get tough. Set her feet on a firm, sure path with You *(Psa. 40:2, 66:9)*. Delight in each step she takes. Direct her confidently *(Psa. 37:23)*. Thank You for giving her power to tread on the enemy and to overcome him in all things *(Luke 10:19)*.

Her Character

A good wife is worth more than jewels. Help her to mature in noble character with our family having full confidence in her. Strengthen her to do our family only good all her life. Give her joy as she serves our family with willing and diligent hands in routine chores. Give her wisdom and grace in all business dealings. Help her to attend well to all the affairs of our household. Give her poise and dignity. Develop in her the inward beauty of a quiet and gentle spirit. May she enjoy the respect of others because the fear of the Lord is upon her life *(Pro. 31:10-31, 1 Pet. 3:4)*.

A Prayer For Our Marriage

Help us both to walk in the light of Jesus, so that we may have unbroken fellowship with You and with one another *(1 John 1:7)*. Enable us to honor You by submitting to each other *(Eph. 5:21)*. Give us patience, faithfulness, and encouragement, and help us to live in complete harmony with the attitude of Christ toward *(Rom. 15:5)*. Keep us both vigilant to guard against any separation of spirit between us.

Let me prize her and love her as Christ loves His bride, the church, and unselfishly give myself for her, so that she might be holy and blameless before You *(Eph. 5:25-28)*. Teach me how to nurture her, cherish her *(Eph. 5:28-29)*, and respect her as a joint-heir of the gift of life in Christ Jesus, so that my prayers will not be hindered *(1 Pet. 3:7)*.

I will not get weary in praying for my wife, my most important responsibility. I will be faithful in it, watching for Your answers and remembering to thank You when they come *(Col. 4:2)*. As I pray for my wife, and as the Holy Spirit helps her, You will cause all things to work together for the good in our family *(Phi. 1:19, Rom. 8:28)*.

I give you all glory in our lives, God, who by Your mighty power at work in us is able to do far more than we could dare to ask or dream — far beyond our highest prayers, desires, thoughts, or hopes *(Eph. 3:20-21)*. In Jesus' name, Amen.

I will walk in integrity in our home *(Psa. 101:2)*.
I accept the Ten Commandments
as God's minimum standard for my life.
1. I will have no other gods before me.
2. I will not serve idols of my own making.
3. I will not misuse the name of God.
4. I will keep the Sabbath holy.
5. I will honor my father and mother.
6. I will not murder.
7. I will not commit adultery.
8. I will not steal.
9. I will not give false testimony.
10. I will not covet anything that belongs to my neighbor.

What If You Are A Single Parent?

Like it or not, a significant percentage of the people who are praying for their families are single parents. The accumulated tasks of wage-earner, parent, housekeeper, etc., weigh heavy on you. Of all those who are praying for their families, you must be the most creative and diligent to carve out time to pray. If you are desperate for help, you will.

Resolve not to talk more about your problems to friends, who have no answers and cannot help, than you take them to God who is the only Answer and is able to do all things well *(Eph. 3:20)*. Here in one volume are some bottom-line, minimum-daily-requirement prayers to build you up and stand with you in the battle for your family.

• Continue to pray for your former mate, and be sure your own heart is clean. The cause of separation is spiritual, not human. Don't forget who the real enemy is.
• Paste these prayers on cards to pray at the breakfast table, or during your lunch hour, and for handy reference in time of need.
• Make a tape of these prayers to play first thing in the morning as you are preparing for the day, or in your car, or as you exercise.
• Ask God for a prayer partner of your same sex, someone who will pray for you daily as they do for their own family.
• Get under the protective covering of authority. This is vitally important. If you are a woman, seek the covering and prayers of your pastor and a male relative — father, brother, uncle, etc. Ask God who. Ask them to ask God if He will confirm to them this role and responsibility. Be sure their wives agree wholeheartedly. If you are a man, be accountable to your pastor and one other man (father, brother, or other respected mature Christian).
• Pray with your children, if they are still at home, and pray more diligently for them if they are not living with you. Remember you only have stewardship of their lives for a little while. Ultimately God is their perfect Father, and He can sovereignly fulfill His plan for their lives *(Psa. 139:16-17)*.

For women especially, remember that God is your perfect Father, Jesus is your perfect Husband, and the Holy Spirit is called the Paraclete, the One who comes alongside to aid, counsel, and comfort *(John 14:16, 15:26, 16:7)*. You are never alone.

Praying For Children

Lord, I prayed for this child, and You have granted me what I asked of You. 1 Samuel 1:27

The assignment to pray for our children is absolutely essential to raise up a generation that will withstand the enemy's attack upon them *(Gen. 22:17, Psa. 127:5)*. These prayers and Scriptures are dedicated to this most important responsibility and privilege.

Lord, what do You want for my children?

Guide me by Your Spirit as I pray for them according to Your will. I release them to You so that You can accomplish Your will for their lives. I will not try to live my life over through them. Keep me from binding them by my needs, wants, and ambitions for them. Get me out of Your way, so that You can work the life of Christ in them and give them Your best. Give me the grace to wait on You, for Your timing is perfect.

I pray that my children will:

1. **Receive and love Jesus as their Savior** — I pray that my children will come to understand that You so loved them that You gave Your only Son for them, that because they believe in Him, they will have life forever with You. *John 3:16*

2. **Commit their lives to make Jesus Lord and be filled with Your Spirit** — I pray that my children will recognize that Jesus is the Name above all names and will confess Him as Lord of all. I pray that they will trust Him with all their heart, not lean on their own understanding, and acknowledge He is Lord in everything; thus, You will guide them in Your best way for them. May they be filled with Your Spirit to the fullness of Christ. *Phi. 2:9-11, Pro. 3:5-6, Eph. 5:18, 1:23, 4:13*

3. **Know the true and living God intimately and cherish and apply all Your names** — I pray that my children will desire to truly know You, Father. May they love You, know You intimately, powerfully apply Your names, and rely on the

character they represent in all their needs. *Dan. 11:32b, Phi. 3:10, Psa. 9:10*

4. **Learn to pray and praise** — I pray that my children will learn to communicate with You, their loving Father. Put Your praise in their hearts and on their lips continually. Lead them to be entirely dependent on You for everything, so they talk with You about all things and give You the honor and glory that You deserve. *Mark 10:14-15, Mat. 21:16, Phi. 4:6*

5. **Know who they are in Christ** — I pray that my children will know how precious they are to You. Teach them to base their identity and security on Christ. Give them Christ-centered confidence and Christ-centered worth. Give them Your mind about how You see them and how You feel about them. As Your creations, help them to fully know who they are and what they have in Christ and what they can do through Him. *Eph. 1:4,7,11-14; Col. 1:27*

6. **Be protected from the evil one by the blood of Jesus** — Protect my children by the covering blood of Jesus. I pray that my children will know the power of the blood to defeat all the works of the evil one. By the blood of Jesus, bind the enemy from interfering with Your perfect purposes in their lives. *John 17:15, 1 John 4:4*

7. **Receive the love of God the Father** — I pray that my children will know Your Father-heart and have the assurance of Your great love. Let them know by experience how extravagantly and unconditionally You love them. Father them with Your holy love, so they know without doubt that You are always working in their lives in Your love. *1 John 3:1*

8. **Love the Word of God** — I pray that my children will treasure Your Word more than wealth. Teach them to love Your Word and base their lives on it as their standard of life. Give them understanding as they humbly seek You in Your Word. Teach them to plead Your unbreakable promises and to defeat all the lies of the enemy with Your truth revealed in Your Word. *Psa. 119:127-130, 159-162*

9. **Learn to hate sin and love holiness, righteousness, and the fear of the Lord** — I pray that You will write Your Word on the hearts of my children, so that they will choose the

obedience of hating sin and loving Your holiness. Work in their lives the holy fear of You and the righteousness of Jesus. Help them not to just keep a set of rules, but to desire to please You in all they do. Create in them a pure heart. Make them wise in what is good and innocent in what is evil. Move in them to dedicate their lives to You as living sacrifices. *Psa. 119:9,11; 2 Tim. 2:22, Rom. 16:19b, Pro. 8:13*

10. **Grow up into maturity in the Lord** — I pray that my children will be built solidly on the foundation of Jesus and grow in Your grace with a conscious sense of Your presence conforming them to be like You. May they continue to be built up with Your wisdom, favor, truth, love, life, faith, strength, and thankfulness. *Luke 2:52, Eph. 4:15, Col. 2:6-7*

11. **Glorify God in their bodies as Your temple** — I pray that my children will honor You by keeping their bodies pure because they are the temple of Your Spirit. Teach them the great price You paid in the death of Jesus for their holiness. *1 Cor. 6:19-20, Rom. 12:1-2*

12. **Respect those in authority** — I pray that my children will submit to the authorities You have placed over them as to You. Let them understand that You have established loving, wise covering for their good through parents and others in authority. Cause them to obey and not reserve for themselves the right to choose to obey, which You call rebellion. Give them a joyful, grateful heart as they submit to Your ordained authorities. *Rom. 13:1, Eph. 6:1, Col. 3:22-25*

13. **Have healthy, edifying, satisfying, wise friendships** — I pray that my children will develop friendships based on the drawing of Your Holy Spirit to righteous companions. Give them friends who are true, wholesome, and mutually encouraging. Give them wisdom in choosing relationships that will honor You. *Psa. 119:63, John 15:13-14*

14. **Know the truth and renew their minds in God's Word** — I pray that my children will know Your truth in their hearts as well as their heads. May they base their life on Your truth instead of Satan's lies, so that they will experience all the freedom that Jesus died to give them. I pray that they will daily renew their minds in Your Word and set their thoughts

on what is true, noble, right, pure, lovely, admirable, excellent, and worthy of praise. *John 8:32, Rom. 12:2, Phi. 4:8*

15. **Walk wisely in the ways and wisdom of God** — I pray that my children will be delighted with Your ways and Your wisdom, that they will commit everything they do to You and trust You to show them the blessings of obedience. Let them not trust in themselves, but put you first in everything. Let their actions reflect the light of Your goodness, righteousness, truth, and wisdom in all they do. Day by day fulfill all Your will for them. *Psa. 37:4-6, Pro. 3:5-6, Eph. 5:8-10, 15-17*

16. **Have the joy of the Lord** — I pray that You alone will be the joy of my children. Fill them with Your joy inside, so they won't pursue the world's pleasure. *Phi. 4:4, Neh. 8:10*

17. **Seek to please God, not self, and serve others** — I pray that my children will desire to please You in their thoughts and actions and not be people-pleasers. May they have servant's hearts and give to others like Jesus who did not seek to be served. *Mat. 4:10b, Psa. 19:14, Mark 10:43-45*

18. **Learn who the enemy is and resist him victoriously** — I pray that my children will humbly submit to God and resist the devil, thereby defeating him. May they discern the evil one's tactics and not entertain his lies in their thoughts nor be entrapped by his snares. I pray that they will receive Your strength and resurrection power for every spiritual battle. *2 Cor. 2:11, Jam. 4:7, Eph. 6:10*

19. **Maintain their first-love devotion to Jesus** — I pray that Jesus will be the first love of my children. Give them a passion for Jesus. Cause them to love Him with all their heart, soul, strength, and mind. I pray that they will prize His affection above all else. *Phi. 3:13-14, Luke 10:27*

20. **Find the godly life partner that God is preparing, a mate who will complement them in their obedient walk with the Lord** — I pray that in Your timing You will bring my children the life partners You have chosen for them. I trust that You are developing the character of Jesus in them. May their walk together with You be an undeniable testimony that You made them for each other. Make them a mighty witness for You. Bless them with Your best. *Pro. 12:4, 31:10; Psa. 112:1-2*
   Amen and Amen.

Seven Blessings For Families

"Come, Holy Spirit, into our greatest needs and give us a revelation of Jesus." This is one of the most effective bottom-line prayers that God has ever taught me to pray for our family.

• **I pray spiritual blessing.** Come, Holy Spirit, give our family a revelation of God as Abba, Father. Give us a love relationship with Jesus so strong that we cannot resist Him. Give us sensitivity to the Holy Spirit and hunger and thirst for righteousness that conforms our conscience to the Word of God. Create in us the fear of the Lord in relation to sin and genuine repentance. Give us holy joy in abiding in You.

• **I pray emotional blessing.** Come, give our family a revelation of Jesus as healer of emotions. Release healing to remove the ground for bondages (rejection, failure, resentment, jealousy, shame, etc.). Let us choose forgiveness for ourselves and others. Give us freedom from fear because God never fails us. Grant us a strong sense of hope to believe God for His promises.

• **I pray mental blessing.** Come, Spirit of truth, and remove blinders of deception from our minds, so that we may know the truth and have godly wisdom and discernment.

• **I pray personal blessing.** Come, give us a sense of our personal value in Christ. Plant in us God-given vision for Your calling on our lives. Give us favor with God and with man.

• **I pray the blessing of right relationship with authority.** Come, teach us submission to God-given authority and counsel. Direct us toward right loyalties, godly soul ties, and healthy friendships that encourage us in our walk with You.

• **I pray physical blessing.** Come, cover us with Your protective hedge of safety, strength, and good health. We plead Psalm 91.

• **I pray financial blessing.** Come, give us Your provision and right relationship to what You give. Let us acknowledge You as our Source and Provider.

I pray blessings. I speak blessings. I choose to be a blessing.

Prayer For Generational Bondages

They overcame the adversary by the blood of the Lamb,
and the word of their testimony ... Rev. 12:11

Father, I confess that my family and I have been bound in generational iniquities of _____, etc. (Ask God to show you.) You are faithful and just to break these bondages and forgive these sins and to cleanse us from all unrighteousness. We have an Advocate, our Savior and Lord Jesus Christ, who pleads our case. All power is in the blood of the Lamb, which sealed our "not guilty" verdict.

In the name of the Lord Jesus Christ and on the basis of His finished work, I take back from the enemy all ground that our family has given him. I reject his influence and cover these areas with the blood of Jesus. In Jesus' name, I renounce all unholy communications and relationships established by the powers of darkness in our family line. In Jesus' name, I bind, cancel, and break all spirits in our family line that are keeping our family in bondage. The enemy has no legal ground in our lives to continue to exploit these generational strongholds, because the power of the cross rendered him legally null and void.

I bring God's Word against the enemy. I submit to God and resist the devil, so he has to flee. The finished work of my Lord Jesus Christ binds powers, principalities, rulers of the darkness, thrones, dominions, and spiritual wickedness in high places. The name and authority of Jesus rebukes, cancels, and nullifies all wicked contracts and assignments of familiar spirits. This is a legal cease and desist order. The enemy cannot win— God contends with those who contend with us.

Captain of the Lord's host, send mighty warrior angels to protect us at the command of Jesus. True and living God, send all curses back to their source. Refer the consequences to the cross of the worthy Lamb of God, who bore them by His sinless sacrifice. We are Your blood-bought children. Send angels to fill up this house, so that nothing can influence us but the power of the living God. Come, Holy Spirit, into our greatest needs and give us a revelation that Jesus is the answer. Speak grace, truth, wisdom, and revelation to us in love. As for me and my house, we will serve the Lord. The Lord Jesus Christ has all authority here. Amen.

Prayer Of Forgiveness For The Family

Thank You, my forgiving heavenly Father, for the mind of Christ that enables me to forgive as You have forgiven me. I place all my expectations on the altar to You. My soul finds rest in God alone; my salvation comes from Him *(Psa. 62:1).* I forgive all offenses of sin, weakness, and failure of _____ (name family member) against me. You created us in Your image, and I choose to forgive _____ for not yet becoming all You created him/her to be. I accept _____ with needs, wounds, and hurts that need the healing that only You can give.

Forgive me for looking to a person to give me the love and affirmation that only Jesus can give. You are my Healer, my Satisfaction, and my Joy, and I will look to You for affirmation. As Jesus enables us to forgive and accept one another, perfect in us His holy character of unconditional love and servanthood. Forgive me for my own selfishness and performance-based acceptance of _____. Love _____ through me.

Enable us to extend grace to each other with unconditional acceptance. Let us choose no longer to strive with one another, demanding change, love, unselfishness, or understanding. Let us truly and freely choose to forgive. A family that is living in freedom consists of good forgivers. Free us from judgment, bitterness, resentment, anger, retaliation, and wall-building. Let us be free to release each other to Your love, power, and purposes.

As God enables me, I will live at peace with _____. His/her wrong actions no longer have permission to wound my spirit. I do not have to react to them, because I choose to take them to the cross of Jesus Christ. I choose to live above anger, unforgiveness, and hurt. Jesus is my Life, and by God's grace working in me, I am an overcomer in His Spirit. I will honor _____ as someone Jesus died for. I will bless _____, giving love that never fails time to do its work. Love through me without reservation with the heart of the Father, the grace of the Son, and the power of the Spirit.

Thank You, loving Father, that I am free in Jesus, seated at Your right hand. I am released to be a channel of Your freedom, forgiveness, and healing love to our family. In Jesus' name, Amen.

Declaration of Release

Make this declaration of release of your family for God to keep that which you have committed to Him *(2 Tim. 1:12)*.

Because Jesus Christ is my Lord, I free you from my anxiety, fears, and control. I place you at God's throne of grace. I cannot impose my will on you. I know that I cannot live your life for you. You are a very special person. As much as I love you, God loves you more.

I have given you back to God the Father, Son, and Holy Spirit. Your life today is totally in His hands, and I trust Him with it. I entrust you to the deposit of God in you for Him to work in you in His time and in His way. I trust the Holy Spirit to draw you and show you the way that is right— the way of love, joy, and peace, and all that salvation includes.

In Jesus' name,
   I give you my blessings,
   I loose you,
   I let you go.
In His love,

I release the following:

Date:

God Is Greater

Our God is an awesome God *(Neh 1:5)*! He is not up for election. He is still on His throne, the already-crowned King of kings *(Psa. 47:2,8)*. He will forever be greater than he that is in the world, and He is in me and my family *(1 John 4:4)*. People are only flesh and blood, while the real enemy is the spiritual forces of wickedness behind the actions. The Good News of the cross of Jesus Christ is that God is powerful enough to defeat the evident works of unrighteousness inspired by the adversary. Jesus is the name above all names, Jehovah-Nissi, our banner of victory. As we lift up the name of the Mighty Warrior, He fights our battles, and we can stand against the enemy *(Exo. 14:14)*. The gates of hell shall not prevail against the name of Jesus as He is lifted up in our otherwise impossible situations. Praise His powerful name, not rehearse the problem and call it prayer.

In the name of the Lord Jesus Christ, and by the power of the Holy Spirit, I lift to the Father our family, myself, our home and work-place, and _____. I plead the blood of the Lord Jesus Christ over all of us. I stand in my righteous, legitimate, delegated authority to declare the names of Jesus, to plant His victory banner to win specific prayer battles against the works of darkness. (Read the following declarations this way: "The God of salvation, the Light of revelation, is greater than darkness, blindness, unbelief, confusion and doubt. Jesus, The True Witness, the Life-Giving Spirit, is greater than deafness, etc ..."

He that is in me	is greater than—
1. God of salvation, Light of revelation	1. darkness, blindness, unbelief, confusion, doubt
2. The True Witness, Life-giving Spirit	2. deafness, hardness of heart, coldness, unteachability
3. Most High God	3. idolatry, going after other gods
4. Spirit of revelation, Author/Finisher of faith	4. religiosity, form of godliness, works, self-righteousness
5. Holy Spirit, Consuming fire	5. hypocrisy, phonyism, image, reputation
6. Holy God, Refiner and purifier	6. sins of the flesh, adultery, lust, fornication, pornography

7.	God our Provider, Abundant life of Jesus	7.	worldliness, love of money, greed, coveting, busyness, ease
8.	Holy Servant Jesus, Spirit of humility	8.	pride, selfishness, haughtiness, mocking, competition
9.	Lord of lords, Lord God Omnipotent	9.	lawlessness, I am my own God, I will do it my way!
10.	All-authority of Jesus, All-sovereign God	10.	rebellion, independent spirit, unsubmissiveness, willfulness
11.	Almighty God, The I AM	11.	control, manipulation, power
12.	God our peace, Lord of life	12.	death, murder, violence, hatred, suicide, anger, destruction
13.	God of all grace, Father of mercies	13.	bitterness, unforgiveness, resentment, criticism, judgment
14.	Trinity unity love, Spirit of repentance	14.	separation, jealousy, irritation, conflict, prejudice, presumption
15.	Spirit of truth, Wisdom of God	15.	lies, denial, deception, futility, resisting counsel, compromise
16.	Redeemer, Deliverer	16.	bondages, addictions, gluttony, compulsiveness
17.	Lord of hosts, Abba, Father	17.	strongholds of disobedience, repeated sin, sins of the fathers
18.	Fear of the Lord	18.	people-pleasing, fear of man
19.	All-sufficient God, God who is there	19.	fear, distrust, anxiety, tension, insecurity, worry
20.	God our Maker, Love of the Father	20.	self-rejection, timidity, self-hatred, withdrawal
21.	Lord my Victory, God of hope	21.	oppression, depression, guilt, condemnation, shame
22.	God my Healer, Comforter	22.	physical infirmity, sickness, pain, emotional woundedness
23.	Cleansing Fire, Healer and Restorer	23.	sexual perversion, incest, homosexuality, sexual abuse
24.	All-sufficient God, Joy of the Lord	24.	ungrateful spirit, murmuring, complaining, criticism

25.	Wonderful Counselor, Spirit of the Lord	25.	human effort, confidence in flesh, human reasoning
26.	Faithful God	26.	lack of discipline, lethargy, procrastination, laziness
27.	Crucified Savior, Overcomer	27.	repeated failure, poverty, lack, defeat, barrenness, infertility
28.	Judge, Word of life	28.	profanity, gossip, slander, idle words, unholy mouth
29.	Jealous God	29.	dishonoring the Lord's day
30.	Spirit of truth, Most High God	30.	occult spirits of darkness and death, error, rock music
31.	Jesus Christ the Lord, True and living God	31.	anti-Christ spirit that does not confess Jesus Christ is Lord

Jesus is greater than spells, curses, voodoo, witchcraft, satanic rituals, bad wishes, soulish prayers, generational sins, weaknesses, character defects, personality traits, inherited disorders, unholy bonds and ties, and every other thing in all creation. Our God is an awesome God. When the sword of the Spirit of truth sets us free, we are free indeed to inherit all that our Father intended for us as children of God. He sends mighty angels to cleanse with His holy authority all areas vacated by the forces of evil. His Holy Spirit fills our bodies, souls, and spirits. Where the Spirit of the Lord is, there is liberty.

He is granting all of us, according to the riches of His glory, to be strengthened with power through His Holy Spirit in our inner man, so that Christ may dwell in our hearts through faith, and that we will be rooted and grounded in love, and be able to comprehend with all the saints what is the breadth, length, height, and depth of the love of Christ which surpasses knowledge, and be filled up to all the fullness of God *(Eph. 3:14-19).*

This is the abridged version of "Lift High The Lord Your Banner" from the Warfare section of **Prayer Portions.**

Under Authority

It has never been more important to be submitted to authority, and it is no more popular now than when Eve substituted her own judgment for God's Word about the forbidden tree. Right relationship to authority begins with submission to God *(James 4:8)*. It includes being under the authority of your pastor, boss, husband, or parents. God commands it *(Rom. 13:2, 1 Pet. 2:13-18)*. Jesus commended it as the way of great faith *(Mat. 8:8-10)*. He said that a Roman soldier who understood authority was nearer the kingdom than the Pharisees who knew all the law.

Submission respects God-appointed authority *(1 Cor. 11:3, 1 Peter 2:17, 3:1-7)* and the husband's headship *(Eph. 5:22-24)*. It is the place of protection where we are safe from unnecessary temptations. God clearly links submission and answered prayer *(1 John 3:21-22)*. Submitting to authority honors them out of reverence for Christ *(Col. 3:18, Eph. 5:21-22)*, recognizing His example of humility and our purpose to be conformed to His image *(Phi. 2:5-8, Rom. 8:28-29)*. It is an attitude of heart by which we choose to put another person's needs, desires, rights, and position ahead of our own *(Eph. 5:21)*. It is the place of grace.

Spiritual leaders need to be accountable. They can be saved from tragic mistakes of pride and greed, if they humble themselves and submit to God-given counsel. King Saul disregarded the word of God through Samuel, and God took the kingdom from him *(1 Sam. 13:8-14)*. King Uzziah disregarded God's delegated authority for offering sacrifice. God characterized him as prideful and unfaithful *(2 Chron. 26:16-21)*. God judged him instantly with leprosy.

Ask God, **"Am I truly submitted to the will of my God-given authorities? By my independent spirit do I reveal that I am my own authority? Do I respect those over me and uphold their known wishes? Am I teachable? Am I controlling?"** We invite needless enemy attack when we step outside God's covering. The consequences in these times are too serious, and the blessings of freedom and protection too precious to do anything less than abide under God-ordained authority. If there is any breach of honor, trust, or respect, make things right today with your pastor, husband, boss, parent, or other covering. You will be blessed as you respect your God-given covering.

When You Don't Know What To Pray— Pray God's Sovereignty

God is sovereign. All authority, all power is His. *Mat. 28:18.*
Nothing takes Him by surprise. All circumstances serve Him. He knows the end from the beginning. *Psa. 119:91, Isa. 46:9-10.*
His word is forever settled in heaven. *Psa. 119:89.*
He does all things for our good and His glory, to conform us to the likeness of Jesus. *Rom. 8:28-29.*
The blood of Jesus covers all circumstances, people, places, and times. The One who did not spare His own Son will freely give us all His best things. *Rom. 8:31-32.*
God is for us and nothing can separate us from His love. That was settled on the cross. *Rom. 8:35-39.*
His lovingkindness never ceases. His compassions never fail. They are new every day. Great is His faithfulness. *Lam. 3:22-23.*
He supplies all our needs by His riches in Jesus. *Phi. 4:19.*
He knows, cares, and numbers the hairs of our heads. *Mat. 10:30.*
He is God of all comfort, Father of mercies. *2 Cor. 1:3-4.*
He is able to supply His abundant grace to us, so that in all things, at all times, we have all of His sufficient grace we need for all encouragement and hope. *2 Cor. 9:8.*
He shows His perfect power in our weakness. *2 Cor. 12:9-10.*
We can know with certainty that He is able to guard what we have entrusted to Him. *2 Tim. 1:12.*
He is our strength, our shield, our strong tower, our refuge, our hope, our joy, our peace, our all. *Psa. 18:1-3, Col. 3:11b.*
He renews our strength as we wait on Him. *Isa. 40:31.*
He will never leave us nor forsake us. He is with us, a very present help. *Heb. 13:5-6, Psa. 46:1.*
He never goes back on a promise. *Josh. 21:45.*
He has a heart that tears can touch and invites us to climb up in the Father's lap and cry. *Heb. 4:15, Psa. 56:8.*
He gives gladness instead of sorrow and praise instead of fainting. Weeping may endure for a night, but He gives the joy that comes in the morning. *Isa. 61:3, Psa. 30:5.*
He is enthroned on the praises of His children. *Psa. 22:3.*
When we lift Him up continually in a sacrifice of praise, we glorify Him here-and-now. *John 12:28a.*

Father, glorify Your name this hour.

Renewing Your Mind In The Word

Effectual intercession depends on seeking the will of God. When we want to pray God's perspective, we start with His Word. As we seek Him in His Word, we can agree with Him in prayer. He hears and answers when we pray His will *(1 John 5:14-15)*.

One effectual plan for a month is **five Psalms and one chapter of Proverbs each day**. This provides daily promises, praises, strength for war, comfort, and wisdom. Use the chart below until you get the hang of adding 30, 60, 90, and 120 to the day of the month. This never gets old as God's eternal word is continually alive and true for new life situations at all times.

Day	Chapter	Chapter	Chapter	Chapter
1	31	61	91	121
2	32	62	92	122
3	33	63	93	123
4	34	64	94	124
5	35	65	95	125
6	36	66	96	126
7	37	67	97	127
8	38	68	98	128
9	39	69	99	129
10	40	70	100	130
11	41	71	101	131
12	42	72	102	132
13	43	73	103	133
14	44	74	104	134
15	45	75	105	135
16	46	76	106	136
17	47	77	107	137
18	48	78	108	138
19	49	79	109	139
20	50	80	110	140
21	51	81	111	141
22	52	82	112	142
23	53	83	113	143
24	54	84	114	144
25	55	85	115	145
26	56	86	116	146
27	57	87	117	147
28	58	88	118	148
29	59	89	119	149
30	60	90	120	150

Evening Prayer For The Home

God set apart the priests to carry the ark of the covenant, to minister to Him, and to bless the people in His name *(Deu. 10:8)*. Upholding the word and presence of God, praising and praying to Him, and blessing His people were the perpetual assignment of priests *(Jer. 33:18)*. We are priests by the blood of the New Covenant with the same charge of continual prayer and blessing *(1 Thes. 5:17, Heb. 13:15)*. Pray this priestly prayer out loud for your family each evening.

Father, as Your priest in this home, I bow before You to worship and adore You. You are all-loving, all-wise, and all-powerful. You are worthy of all honor, praise, and glory. I come to you in Jesus' name and by the sacrifice of His atoning blood which covers our sins this day. As I confess my sins of _____, You are faithful and just to forgive me of sin and cleanse me of all unrighteousness. Thank You for Your mercy. I am clothed in the righteousness of the worthy Lamb and anointed with the oil of Your Spirit. You have blessed me with every spiritual blessing, authority, and strength in Christ Jesus.

I present our family to You, as the priest of our home. Thank You for the protection of the precious blood of Jesus covering us, our property, and our possessions against the schemes of the enemy to steal, kill, and destroy. You have clothed us in the full armor of the Lord Jesus to withstand all the flaming missiles of the enemy. The blood of Jesus is between my family and all evil footholds of the enemy, which we may have invited by ignorance or disobedience. Break the power of any soulish prayers that have been offered for any of us not in Your perfect will. In Jesus' name, I command the enemy to leave this home. Send mighty warring angels to surround us, dismiss all enemy assignments, and protect us from harm *(Psalm 91)*.

Fill our household with Your Spirit, so that sin has no dominion here. Minister your love, joy, and peace to us. You are our rear guard throughout the night *(Isa. 52:12)*. Bless us with refreshing and renewing sleep to awake to a new day of Your plans for us. Thank You for the assurance of Your covenant of faithfulness to us. Draw us closer to You, give us a passion for Jesus, and bless us to fulfill Your highest purposes. Thank You for the right and privilege of protecting my family by this prayer offered in Jesus' name, Amen.

Psalm 91

Psalm 91 is called the Soldier's Psalm. We are told that in World War I, the soldiers of the 91st Brigade recited the 91st Psalm daily. This brigade engaged in three of the war's bloodiest battles. Other units suffered up to 90% casualties, but the 91st Brigade did not suffer a single combat-related death. God is willing and able to keep His words of covenant promise. Plead God's shield daily in these evil times. We confidently claim His rest, refuge, safety, covering, faithfulness, freedom from fear, angelic watchers, deliverance, and protection. Memorize it, meditate on it, and pray it out loud for your family. It could mean the difference between life and death!

[1] He who dwells in the shelter of the Most High will rest in the shadow of the Almighty. [2] I will say of the Lord, "He is my refuge and fortress, my God, in whom I trust."
[3] Surely He will save you from the fowler's snare and from the deadly pestilence. [4] He will cover you with His feathers, and under His wings you will find refuge; His faithfulness will be your shield and rampart.

[5] You will not fear the terror of night, nor the arrow that flies by day, [6] nor the pestilence that stalks in the darkness, nor the plague that destroys at midday.
[7] A thousand may fall at your side, ten thousand at your right hand, but it will not come near you. [8] You will only observe with your eyes and see the punishment of the wicked.

[9] If you make the Most High your dwelling— even the Lord, who is your refuge— [10] then no harm will befall you, no disaster will come near your tent.
[11] For He will command His angels concerning you to guard you in all your ways; [12] they will lift you up in their hands, so that you will not strike your foot against a stone. [13] You will tread upon the lion and the cobra; you will trample the great lion and the serpent.

[14] "Because he loves me," says the Lord, "I will rescue him; I will protect him, for he acknowledges my name. [15] He will call upon me, and I will answer him; I will be with him in trouble, I will deliver him and honor him. [16] With long life I will satisfy him and show him my salvation."